P9-CRF-698

South American Animals
Howler Monkeys

Big Buddy BOOKS
South American Animals

ABDO
Publishing Company

by Julie Murray

VISIT US AT
www.abdopublishing.com

Published by ABDO Publishing Company, PO Box 398166, Minneapolis, Minnesota 55439.

Copyright © 2014 by Abdo Consulting Group, Inc. International copyrights reserved in all countries. No part of this book may be reproduced in any form without written permission from the publisher. Big Buddy Books™ is a trademark and logo of ABDO Publishing Company.

Printed in the United States of America, North Mankato, Minnesota.
092013
012014

 PRINTED ON RECYCLED PAPER

Coordinating Series Editor: Rochelle Baltzer
Editor: Marcia Zappa
Contributing Editors: Megan M. Gunderson, Sarah Tieck
Graphic Design: Maria Hosley
Cover Photograph: *Getty Images*: Mark Bowler.
Interior Photographs/Illustrations: *Getty Images*: Enrique R. Aguirre (p. 11), Joel Sartore (p. 25); *Glow Images*: Arco Images (p. 19), Juniors Bildarchiv (p. 19), © Kevin Schafer/Corbis (p. 5), Jurgen & Christine Sohns/FLPA (p. 29); *iStockphoto*: ©iStockphoto.com/OGphoto (p. 7), ©iStockphoto.com/JohanSjolander (p. 4), ©iStockphoto.com/WishingWell (p. 23); *Minden Pictures*: © Thomas Marent (p. 13), © Piotr Naskrecki (p. 21), © Pete Oxford (p. 27), © Kevin Schafer (p. 17); *Science Source*: Francois Gohier (p. 15), B. G. Thomson (p. 11); *Shutterstock*: Ammit Jack (p. 4), Jules_Kitano (p. 8), LeonP (p. 9), Vadim Petrakov (p. 9).

Library of Congress Cataloging-in-Publication Data

Murray, Julie, 1969- author.
  Howler monkeys / Julie Murray.
    pages cm. -- (South American animals)
  Audience: 7 to 11.
  ISBN 978-1-62403-189-2
  1. Howler monkeys--Juvenile literature. I. Title.
  QL737.P915M87 2014
  599.8'55--dc23
                        2013025491

Contents

Long ago, nearly all land on Earth was one big mass. About 200 million years ago, the land began to break into **continents**. One of these is South America.

Howler monkeys are named for their loud calls. They can be heard from miles away!

South America includes several countries and **cultures**. It is known for its rain forests and interesting animals. One of these animals is the howler monkey.

Howler Monkey Territory

There are many different types of howler monkeys. They live in northern South America and Central America. Central America is the southern part of North America.

Howler monkeys live in rain forests. These forests are usually warm, wet, and thick with plants.

Howler Monkey Territory

Uncovered!
Howler monkeys are a type of New World monkey. New World monkeys are found in Central and South America. Old World monkeys are found in Asia and Africa.

Howler monkeys spend almost their whole lives in trees.

7

Welcome to South America!

If you took a trip to where howler monkeys live, you might find…

S O U T H

P A C I F I C

…different languages.

Portuguese and Spanish are the most common languages spoken in South America. Many people also speak Dutch, French, and English. And, there are many local languages. One local name for the howler monkey is *barrigudo*, which means "big belly."

Cape Horn

...New World monkeys.

Howler monkeys aren't the only monkeys in South America. Other New World monkeys include capuchins (*right*), marmosets, night monkeys, squirrel monkeys, and tamarins.

...towering waterfalls.

Two of the world's highest waterfalls are in Venezuela in northern South America. At Angel Falls (*right*), the water drops 3,212 feet (979 m)! And at Cuquenán Falls, the water drops 2,000 feet (610 m).

Take a Closer Look

Howler monkeys have sturdy arms and legs. They have special tails that can be used to **grip**. A howler monkey's face has two big eyes, a nose, and a thin mouth.

Howler monkeys have long, thick fur. It can be many colors including black, brown, reddish, and tan. Different types of howler monkeys are often recognized by their fur color.

Many howler monkeys have beards growing from their chins. Males usually have longer beards than females.

A howler monkey's furry tail has a bare spot underneath the tip. This helps it hold on to branches.

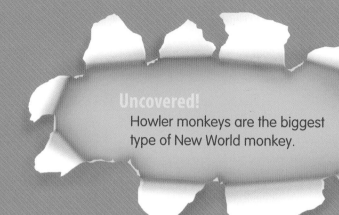

Uncovered!
Howler monkeys are the biggest
type of New World monkey.

Adult howler monkeys are 15 to 48 inches (38 to 122 cm) long. Their tails are another 19 to 36 inches (48 to 91 cm) long. They weigh 6.5 to 25 pounds (3 to 11 kg). Males are larger than females.

The Guatemalan black howler monkey is one of the largest types of howler monkeys. It is also called the Yucatán black howler monkey.

Social Life

Howler monkeys live in groups called troops. A troop usually has 10 to 20 members. But, it may have as few as 2 or as many as 45!

Each troop has its own home area. Home areas are usually smaller than 79 acres (32 ha).

Sometimes, the home areas of different troops include shared land. But, troops try to stay away from each other. If they meet, the males may fight.

Troop members include males, females, and young.

15

Howler monkeys spend their days with their troop. They eat together and **groom** each other. They also spend a lot of time resting. They sleep on branches near their troop members.

Howler monkeys rarely come down from the treetops. They slowly move through the branches. And, they stick together as a troop. An old male member often leads the group.

Uncovered!
Howler monkeys can swim.

Because they live high in trees, howler monkeys have few natural predators. Their predators include jaguars and large snakes and birds.

Booming Voices

Uncovered!
In areas with few howler monkeys, calls are less common. Monkeys with plenty of space between troops only howl a few times a week.

Howler monkeys are known for their loud calls. These howls can be heard as far as three miles (5 km) away!

Howler monkeys call to let other troops know where they are. This helps troops stay away from each other and avoid fighting. They often howl when the sun rises and sets. They also howl before and during rainstorms or when they are disturbed.

Some people think a howler monkey's call sounds like a lion's roar.

Male howler monkeys (*right*) have louder, more individual calls than females (*left*).

19

A howler monkey is well built for calling loudly. It has a large neck and lower **jaw**.

Inside its neck is a big, shell-shaped **organ**. Air moves through this organ. It makes a howler monkey's calls loud and carry long distances.

Howler monkeys make sounds other than just howls. These include barks and grunts.

21

Mealtime

Howler monkeys find different foods in their treetop homes. They mostly eat leaves. But, they also eat flowers, nuts, and fruits. They especially like figs.

Uncovered!

Howler monkeys get almost all of the water they need from their food. They only come to the ground to find water when the weather is especially dry.

The food that howler monkeys eat does not provide much energy. That is why these monkeys move slowly and rest a lot.

Baby Monkeys

Howler monkeys are **mammals**. Females usually have one baby at a time. A newborn is small and light colored. It drinks its mother's milk and grows.

Howler monkey mothers guard their babies closely. Males, even fathers, may try to kill the babies.

At first, a baby howler monkey holds on to its mother's belly. After a while, it rides on her back. Later, a baby begins to follow its mother through the treetops. At one to one and a half years old, it is ready to live without its mother's help.

Female troop members give baby howler monkeys a lot of attention. Sometimes, they help a mother raise her baby.

When riding on its mother's back, a baby howler monkey holds on with its arms, legs, and tail.

Survivors

Life in South America isn't easy for howler monkeys. People hunt them. New buildings and farms take over their **habitats**. And, sicknesses harm them.

Still, these monkeys **survive**. People work to make sure they have safe areas to live freely. Howler monkeys help make South America an amazing place!

The Guatemalan black howler monkey and the Maranhão red-handed howler monkey are endangered. This means they are in great danger of dying out.

In the wild, howler monkeys live for 15 to 20 years.

Wow!
I'll bet you never knew...

...that only New World monkeys, such as howler monkeys, can use their tails to hold things.

...that howler monkeys are the loudest type of monkey in the world. And, they are the loudest type of New World animal!

...that howler monkeys can be very hard to locate in the wild. Their calls are so loud, it may sound like they are nearby. But they may actually be far away!

Important Words

continent one of Earth's seven main land areas.

culture (KUHL-chuhr) the arts, beliefs, and ways of life of a group of people.

grip to hold tightly.

groom to clean and care for.

habitat a place where a living thing is naturally found.

jaw a mouthpart that allows for holding, crushing, and chewing.

mammal a member of a group of living beings. Mammals make milk to feed their babies and usually have hair or fur on their skin.

organ a body part that does a special job. The heart and the lungs are organs.

survive to continue to live or exist.

Web Sites

To learn more about howler monkeys, visit ABDO Publishing Company online. Web sites about howler monkeys are featured on our Book Links page. These links are routinely monitored and updated to provide the most current information available.

www.abdopublishing.com

Index